Simple Machines

Gare Thompson

Contents

Work

What does **work** mean to a scientist? Scientists say that work is done when a **force** is used to move an object over a distance. To do work, you must move something.

Suppose you use force to push on a wall. Are you doing work? No, the wall does not move. What if you push a door and it opens. Now, you are doing work. The door moved. Your push was the force that made the door move.

Planting a tree is work. You push the tree into the soil. The tree has moved into its new home.

Machines and Work

We do work each day. But we can make work easier. How? We can use machines. A **machine** is anything that helps us do work. Machines make work easier. They help us cut things, mix things, and move heavy things. Some machines are called simple machines. A **simple machine** is a machine that has few or no moving parts.

A simple machine does one of the following:

- Increases the speed of something
- Increases the force that you use
- Changes the direction of the force that you use

Let's look at how simple machines help us do work.

Scissors are a machine. They make it easier to cut paper.

The Six Kinds of Simple Machines

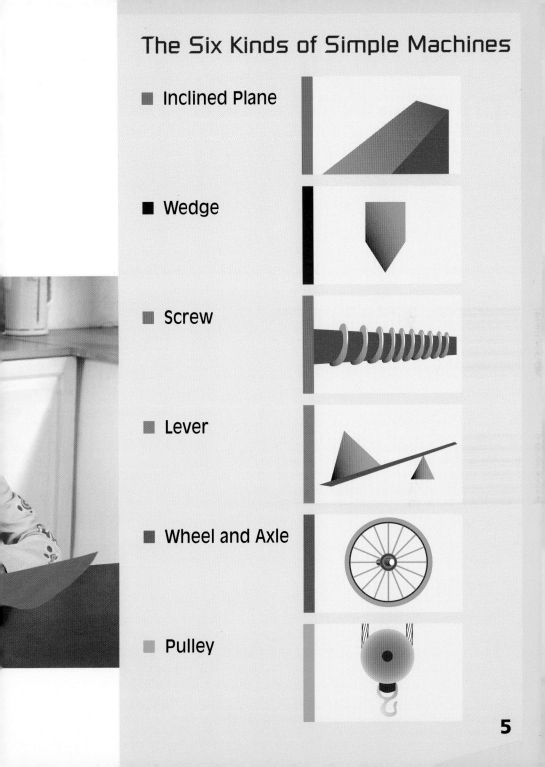

- Inclined Plane

- Wedge

- Screw

- Lever

- Wheel and Axle

- Pulley

The Inclined Plane

You need to put a large heavy box in the back of a truck. You can't lift it. The box is too heavy. There must be some way to move the box. You see a board. Could you push the box up the board? Yes, that would be easier than lifting it.

You place one end of the board on the ground. You place the other end on the back of the truck. You push the box up into the back of the truck. You use the board as a ramp.

The ramp is a simple machine called an **inclined plane**. This simple machine doesn't move, but it helps you move things. With an inclined plane, you can move objects with less force.

How We Use Inclined Planes

Look around you and you will see many inclined planes in use. Look for these simple machines when you cross the street. Look for them when you enter buildings in your town. Where else can you see people using inclined planes?

Inclined planes are built to make it easier for people to move around.

Machines Long Ago

The Inclined Plane

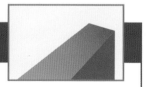

We are not sure how the pyramids in Egypt were built. One idea is that the Egyptians used inclined planes or ramps. The workers pushed the heavy stones up the ramps.

The Wedge

Did you know you use a simple machine every time you cut a sandwich? A knife is a simple machine called a **wedge**. You push down on the knife. The downward force causes the bread to split.

How We Use Wedges

A wedge is used to split or cut things. A wedge can be broad and flat like a knife or an ax. A wedge can also be round and pointed like an arrow.

An ax is a heavy wedge. To split wood, you swing the ax downward. The downward force is changed into a sideways force. The sideways force pushes the wood apart.

Nearly all cutting tools use the wedge.

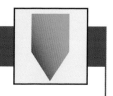

Machines Long Ago

The Wedge

Farmers used to use simple wooden or metal plows pulled by farm animals to dig their fields. A plow is a type of wedge. As a plow is dragged along, it cuts the ground, pushing the soil aside. Today many farmers use machines powered by engines to do this work.

Sometimes simple machines are combined to do work. The zipper uses the idea of both the inclined plane and the wedge. The zipper's slide has wedges that open and close the teeth.

Speaking of teeth, did you know that you have wedges in your body? Remember that most wedges are cutting tools. What part of your body do you use to cut things? That's right, your front teeth are wedges!

When you bite into an apple, your front teeth act as wedges.

The Screw

You want to put a shelf in your room. You have a board and a bracket. And you have something else. You have another simple machine called a **screw**. You can use the screw to attach the bracket to the wall. Then you can hang up your shelf.

Look at the picture of a screw. See the curves going around the screw? The ridges that stick out on a screw are called **threads**. A screw is really an inclined plane that has been twisted in a circle.

◀ body

◀ threads

The end of a light bulb is a kind of screw.

Remember that moving something up an inclined plane takes less force than lifting it straight up. A screw is a twisted inclined plane. So when you turn a screw, you use less force than if you tried to push the screw straight into the wall.

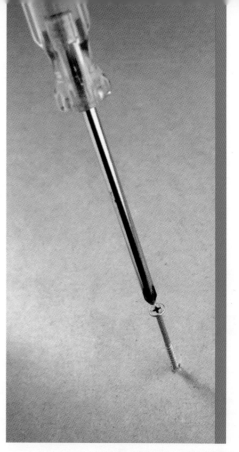

The threads on a screw make it easier to put a screw into a wall.

Machines Long Ago

The Screw

Long ago, a Greek scientist named Archimedes invented a lifting screw. It helped farmers water their crops. The lifting screw moved water from a lower level to a higher level. It had a crank attached to a screw. When a farmer turned the crank, water went up the screw and then spilled out.

How We Use Screws

Screws do more than just hold things together. Screws can be used to make holes. A drill is a machine that uses a screw. This machine drills into wood. The screw moves in and out of the wood. This makes a hole in the wood.

A drill uses a kind of screw to make a hole in wood quickly and easily.

The Lever

The **lever** is another kind of simple machine. A lever is a bar that can be used for lifting. Look at the girl in the picture. She's using the stick as a lever. She puts the stick under a heavy rock. The rock is the **load**, or the object she wants to move. Then she balances the stick on a small rock. The small rock acts as a **fulcrum**. A fulcrum lets a lever change the direction of a force. So when the girl pushes down on the stick, the heavy rock is pushed up.

▼force

fulcrum ▶

▲ load

How We Use Levers

Levers help us do work. We use levers to move heavy loads. We use levers to pry or crack things open. Levers also help us have fun. We use levers when we play baseball or ride on a seesaw.

A lever helps us do work by changing the direction of the force we use. To move the rock up, the girl pushed down on the stick. A lever can also change the amount of force we use. The girl used less force to push down on the stick than she would use if she lifted the rock straight up.

Every lever can change the direction of a force. But levers can look very different. A baseball bat is a lever. A pair of scissors has two levers that share one fulcrum.

Machines Long Ago

The Lever

Some scientists think that the lever was the first machine humans used. Early people used tree branches to move huge rocks. The tree branch was the lever. Another rock was the fulcrum. Where did the force come from?

A bat is a lever that helps you hit a ball really hard.
Your hands are the bat's fulcrum.

The Wheel and Axle

Wheels are all around us. How did you get to school today? Did you ride a bike or take a bus? If you did, then you used a **wheel** and **axle**.

The wheel and axle is a simple machine with two parts, a wheel and an axle. The wheel turns on a post called an axle. Watch a bike wheel spin. Does it fly off the bike when it spins? No, the wheel stays on the bike because it spins on an axle. The wheel and axle work together.

Machines Long Ago

The Wheel

Some scientists say that the wheel is the most important invention of all time. Long ago, wheels were used to make pottery. Wheels are used in almost every machine that helps us travel from place to place.

axle

wheel

How We Use Wheels and Axles

Some machines have parts that move up and down. Other machines have parts that move in and out. Many have parts that move in circles. These machines have wheels.

We use the wheel and axle in many different ways. Here is an example of the wheel and axle at work. Can you spot the wheel and axle?

In-line skates have wheels and axles.

The Pulley

Have you ever raised or lowered a flag? Well, if you have, you have used another simple machine. You have used a **pulley**. What does a pulley remind you of? Did you guess a wheel? Let's see how a pulley uses a wheel to make work easier.

A pulley is a wheel that has a rope wrapped around it. A pulley changes the direction of a force. With a pulley, you pull down to lift something up. This can make work easier. It's easier to pull down than it is to lift up.

Some pulleys use two wheels instead of one. With these pulleys you still pull down to lift an object up. But using two wheels lets you use less force. The more wheels you use, the less force you have to use to lift an object.

How We Use Pulleys

Pulleys make our life easier. People use a simple pulley to move things that are hard to reach. Remember the flagpole. It's easier to raise a flag using a pulley than it is to climb a tall ladder.

Construction workers use pulleys to lift heavy loads.

Machines Long Ago

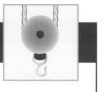

The Elevator

In 1854, Elisha Otis invented the modern safety elevator. This elevator used a series of pulleys to move carloads of people up and down in tall buildings. Unlike earlier elevators, the Otis elevator had a safety device that stopped the elevator from falling if the rope broke.

Glossary

axle a rod that a wheel moves around

force a push or pull

fulcrum a fixed point on which a lever turns to change the direction of a force

inclined plane a simple machine in the shape of a slope that makes moving objects up or down easier

lever a simple machine made of a bar that turns on a fixed point

load an object or weight that is moved

machine something that makes work easier

pulley a simple machine made of a rope or belt that moves over one or more wheels

screw a simple machine that is an inclined plane turned in a circle

simple machine a machine that has few or no moving parts

threads the ridges on a screw

wedge a simple machine that makes cutting or splitting an object easier

wheel a round frame that spins around an axle

work when a force is used to move an object over a distance

Index